THE
UNINHABITABLE

Sibling Rivalry Press, LLC
PO Box 26147
Little Rock, AR 72221
info@siblingrivalrypress.com
www.siblingrivalrypress.com

ISBN: 978-1-943977-57-4

Library of Congress Control No. 2018960665

This title is housed permanently in the Rare Books and Special Collections Vault of the Library of Congress.

First Sibling Rivalry Press Edition, March 2019

THE
UNINHABITABLE

JESSE RICE-EVANS

SIBLING RIVALRY PRESS
DISTURB / ENRAPTURE
LITTLE ROCK / ARKANSAS

TABLE OF CONTENTS

FOR SICK & DISABLED FEMMES EVERYWHERE

I have flung my body away from my body:

echo, heartache, throb beneath bicep, anchor.

Nothing came back in a green glass bottle stoppered with wax
because the internet is not the ocean.

I can forgive the abandonment but I cannot forget the smell,
my skin and skull becoming uninhabitable, propranolol numbing
my bottom lip.

Ask again, and I will tell it to you.

PART I:
GENESIS

Muffle

I never did an especially good job of self-care. Not when I could
do cocaine instead, or tequila, or bong rips. Even after I quit all
those, I waited tables, clanked around the diner for nine hours at a
time, my feet quietly flattening. I moved to New York and walked
everywhere. Not that I'm caught up figuring out who to blame,
or how

My first day on meds I am fluttery, a cave of feathers, meeting
you off Canal Street, iced coffee beading down my wrists, sheen
of sweat a deciduous film, magic husk to keep out urgency; it's
just that now when I make choices for the years still to bloom,
I have to think about how my body will bend or give without
emptying, a sinkhole of aches and moods, a molting

There is a grimness to futurity, a morbidity at the promise of
an end, a slow getting there; we learn to ache in our own ways;
tender spots dapple my ribs, my thighs, my sisterbody one
drenched with fatigue muffled

BONE STUFF

It hurts to listen to women talk around me; it was something my
body swallowed, guzzling stress in my skull, ricocheting around
my body, a long fragment of emotivity, seared and blistering at
the ends, fraying wire crackling against the air around me. This
was my body for so long, I didn't feel it start and I certainly didn't
expect its devolution into abject, withered muscle, seizing carpal
spasmodic.

Again and again I hear *sacrifice* but I know it isn't

Again and again I hear *wound* but I know it isn't

except leaving room for mistakes, courtesy patience virtuous in
ways made long, you keep trying but not finding the ways to keep
me close

We don't do *gentle* like we used to
but what is

maybe a leaf or a feathered ivory
dog peering out of a wicker basket
on the A train, blinking slowly, or the
fluff of my bronzing hair after a hot shower;

a gross blanket, a swimming fossil

Orthopedist slinking in to begin my week, pool of calendar days
to drown in, a holiday sparking a manic episode but in dreams
everything is smooth-edged and gentle, a classroom blooming
eager blossoms, blood thrilling up my throat, spine beckons

THE POOL

The first cool day, I drape my knotted body with old sweatshirt,
cheap canvas sneakers, a dressing down I usually reserve for home;

My period 8 days late, I am crying on the steering wheel, unable
to allow myself to mourn my shoulders, how they escalate, how
I need to pierce myself and drain the excess I am trying everyday
to shove inside my skin like a sack of grains but, you know, the
rotting kind.

I buy makeup that promises *glow* or *glimmer* or another adjective I
reserve for how fireflies were the only lanterns I knew for the first
hundred years of my country life, how everything smelled electric
and benches were jaunty wooden stumped hunks and how your
porch leapt when it saw me drifting.

Instead of glow, I gloom, dark but iridescent dunked gasping,
my body on mute except the dreams where I open drawers of
my dresser from college: cat-eye sunglasses, femme gear, things I
haven't touched since I started to feel;

In another, I am folding laundry still dewy with sunrise, the
hammock a knotted metaphor for my clasped back, how I only
jumped off of the roof that once, mattress leafed with autumn
sparking bark, my legs collapsing into the swell of soft, my own
swells still steeping along my hips, my hands, your hair, hideous
fist I begged you to leave rattling in the pickup bed.

GENESIS

begins in my rumbling mouth full of slip gunk and flipped chairs,
the shot I ripped from yr room and tumbled down a stair my heel

cracking my elbow clenched into stone jumble, hallowed once now
trussed and left behind; You knew where I left knots before, how

I pulled them out of my lavender hair extended drain gulping
habitat, french unbutton, the unlined pocket beside doorknob full

of what you didn't say but thought one thousand times; *Something* isn't
always the right word, but I feel something like panic and engulfed

by it when they became your flinching cavern haunter, your draped
fang, shadowed pine; Your version of love is always cracking,

you need someone to fill you in, curve underneath you to catch
your shards, the few you peel off yourself and the rest that flake

dirt in dry sun. I have to leave to still enjoy the night, the screen
door between me and all my ugly, film of mesh no disguise but

instead protective, a takedown of doubt that you have yet to
shape; days pass without a new photo of you, the corner gay

bars empty and fill like lungs, you don't know what to carry
to disguise you in the world but you want to be there anyway

PART II:
THE UNINHABITABLE

I am knee-deep in rosemary, flowering editorial
My bedroom leaks camphor and anise, warm roots rooting

No one needs another memoir abt a white girl
but here we are, my whiteness a neutrality I can fade into, dozens
of shades of me lining all public, all trenched, worming through
downtown tasseled or flat, texture an afterthought.

As long as men's narratives are *courageous* I purge here and in
the street, behind buildings no longer mine, jewel. Glass shawl
knotted in bodega bag, my mouth unhooked like a flag

are we so neutral as to be blank, all others figures cast over the
draped sheet, objective backdropcloth wrinkled with violence? In
an instant, we erase by refusing to acknowledge an other,
a dynamic character outside of our collective self

I can barely stand how vast you wanted me to be, stretch
gargantuan, thinning, edges tearing like dough, passive as a stretch

HYPOMANIA

Rebirth is just an awful edge, sawtooth, tasting the city I'm left
with. You knew forgiveness was distant, criminal, polymorphing
embryonic, but I demand it anyway, so in-yr-face these days I
barely recognize my shadow. Remind me again to destroy this
thing I've hung from my shoulders, scapula winging but mostly
taut. Treat me like an obstacle: I give you a chance to love me, but
badly, like I've been left out overnight

What it Feels Like

wavering skin and flowered cheek, moves are more like ripples
than anything, the whole sweet gasp a jumped front, wash of low
pressure pulled up on my phone, charcoal crepe blazer across my
gnarled base, tender points
bloom behind my arms, my wings a sinking hunk,
forbidden crease.

somber wracked with eyebrows dripping
forgiveness, the place I've always looked
from, poked tongue into, scraping   or   excavating

I'll wait before you let me drench, the part of me
slaking woman, curdling manicured autumn nails, sleek
jumper, forgettable mug of wine.

The way I save myself and leave my self behind
shredded into photos and didn't even strap
into the backseat or how I cried driving after too many
hours alone with my own voice how I beg
silent how I destroy my bodies boys or fluid or
drenched or tucked under an afghan stoned and
looking forward to me which is why I couldn't
slip away, why I won't happen the way I promised
so even good I am alone or broken or probably without bend.

BETTER SKIN

after Crater

You are so far behind me, gentleness
distance, I forget flat housefronts, etch
and slat, something gnarled or drench
or both but longing drapes everywhere
so forget your queened lament your marbled
spine your wrench shoulder;

If I can't get over you, I will
dive & roll back in at your feet, jetsam.

I cry at the head of the table, my heart
scraped into the wood of your husked hips,
the table we altared and shaped green
intricate brain coral ridge a light before   outage

The new thing is: *having a body is weird*
and it is but yours is fine it is not always
grieving its own slow decay I mean it is but
it also brims with joy and calm and things other
than pain try wearing mine here try it on I'll wait

A Conditional

Something about gladness is grimmer than ever, but the shells we
stole will still rim our neighborhoods, the tweezers I gulped to
find the love of my life drenched in driveway, shrunk into bonds
we failed even the things we said we loved lied humongous.

When shake snuffs haunt, it's okay to remember that I am here
and will stay with you, a crust of tarragon shrimping our nest,
waft relentless, make happy but forgive fast except for some
things, you know the ones: the ugly but you already gave us
incense, beaded truth rippling with yawning breeze so before;

Say what you believe in out loud into my mouth and I will grant
your every thing.

We were burning long before you thought we were, fish-lipped
gridlock drenched quiet: what are you thinking on the silent
train? Working to grin, trudging Thursday, my god they're
everywhere.

I felt looser after, like the way I fell into sleep, crystalline, was less
temporary, my body less of a tomb, more lagoon, more brackish
gulf. I knew before, the way time drips a storm

Rain, Glitter, Rain

after Frank Ocean

You kept looking at me like you wanted to touch me

I thought it would be worse: the seams of my body
tearing in secret, an addendum unfiled, unfiltered

The way my body hurts doesn't require anything from you
means nothing   needs nothing
is like that long wailing whale sound, only from inside me, and
sliced into fragments thinner than a tooth, but just as wary and
vibrating at a frequency you can't touch, spiralling, but too slowly
to even notice, a broken orbit, an okay metaphor for
the stretching and thinning
is rain
is glitter
is rain

Not always pretty, but full of tongues and girls and whichever
slices of me you'd like to see, the same crimped guts you've come
to expect, the shaded swirl, something ruined about my face:

I wanted to be cornered

CERVICAL TRACTION/SUB-OCCIPITAL RELEASE

I'm in my big dream, big woken snuff blood bitch blood filling
the tough sink linoleum, mopped into a sprawl, a yawn of blood,
a yelp in me inside of me in side like I've been folded inside out
and if I dip my finger into my own blood I feel it behind my knees
eyes unctuous AF;

I post about it on the internet and write about it, cycle of set of
behaviors I drool over, flaming blood into magic saliva salivating
delineating haunch or glimpse or you at the end of a long wooden
table eating pretzels and kissing me oh don't stop kissing me

I go to physical therapy my physical therapist is small with hot dry
hands that don't shake even a little bit he seems sturdy and he believes
that my shoulder blades can touch each other if I try hard enough he
says *your left elbow is swollen trycing it sorry try icing it* but it's winter so
why would I ice the frozen meat of my body, the wool coat I dragged
off a rack on Lexington and pulled around my shoulder like a cape,
$20 cashmere in a dry cleaner bag, the wool the only warm thing.

I try on my new clothes, they are supposed to already fit me and I am
supposed to feel at home and I do but I am inconsistent, aggressive,
everyone tells me and I sort of already know but definitely struggle
to care bc if I weren't a femme would it matter my demeanor would
it matter to anyone how much space I need between my thighs on the
crowded 4 train how I could turn my neck 360 degrees then could
stretch this rubber band long AF like a rainbow in front of my chest,
arcing in then yawning out, again, and, again,

ARGONAUT

To empty feels good, to purge interior of self, something warm
gushing forth, a surge of possessiveness, of jealousy for what
shapes my body could take, before my edges grew smudged. Any
answer will erase us, I am not alone in this vanishing, how when I
walk from the train to my college everyone's eyes slide across me,
I am a darkness, a gap between other things to look at.

With my cane, I am a vanishing act. With my fat body, I am
strangely small; my queer haircut summons no mutters of *dyke*,
of *reckless* or *unforgivable*. With my Southern throat,

they said that everything I make will be an analog of my self.

Who knew

we are not made whole by pain, no matter what they say. We
are broken by it, taught to peel back cushion between us and the
world because we have no choice but to rebuild it, again, and, again,

Then You See It

after Rihanna

Is there any additional personal or family medical history?

The first time I see the Pacific, I remember that there is no work
that is not wet work, lamplight a fever, your armpits dampened
improbable and fabulous, rivulets of sequins, nonviolence a lost
prophecy, around and drenched.

Have you ever been hospitalized?

Not really sure how to feel about it, something in the way it
moves: oceanic, but not Atlantic, not the sea I swallowed in early
morning, body slick as seals, parched with Camel Lights, the once
dream sliced up, stowed

Have you ever thought about hurting yourself?

The reason I hold on: 'cause I need this whole gone, when I could
fill you in I promised I could cave and I did, an avalanche of
myself as if I wasn't too much already

Have you ever been treated for alcohol or drug use or abuse?

I want you to stay; Forget the haunches promises or wharfs,
the towel damp on upholstered back seats in Ford Taurus, trees
receded I know when I am trash, a blade in jumpsuit and blazer
too-tight through shoulders, through arms. These are gifts:
roadmap towards immolation, a closing: Whose blood is that?
How did you find me here? I just want to be alive that's it

PART III:
MURMUR

Roseglow

Summer's not as long as it used to be
— Frank Ocean

If every breath is a new beginning, I am tired, sun plummeting
into fist of indigo. The places you used to take me shake dust,
astroturf landing crumbling freckles of plastic, your sneakers
lipped with glitter raining from demolition aftercare.

You work through your worst night, an icon of unreadable past
lives, new names cresting your clothes, new self-smell, sheen of
freshly-waxed drop train, a sleek skin to peel or sport.

All my life, an echo, an unknowable gulf of connective tissue,
the disease I was promised and didn't get

Who knew how weird I were, I dreamt of weird but wasn't it,
wasn't drenched the way I should have been, the way I thrum
medicated, your hands sweating into my clothes, unseasonable
linens, the skirt you can see right through, my knees scalding, the
moment I learn to write again, words are clean splashed across
subway tile in every station, the stop and start of my scraped
brain, a tremor, a tumor, not a tumor, a trembling unforgivable.

It's pretty sweet when you think: I can get free air above ground,
my body carries it through tunnels and the slow crawl of my body
in the tubes, a virtual in-front-of-you-ness, a former visibility
that stops mattering when it devastates my throat. I can cut
through any quiet, any hole you sought solace in is now mine

because I am ruthless. If you wanted a sad, you're looking wrong,
looking okay doing it in sleeveless black tee, a sleek look, droplets
speckling from your drenched head, dry sweater below.

Less sorrow, more sharp, shaping sharpness is a hobby, a round
thing desperate to get sleek, edged, softness closing in to become
hard, my hair tumbling into the stained toilet bowl, rainbow
of copper left over from summer; this purge marks the end of
something, a new edge to peruse or embody or something

DRAWL

Twilight, I sprawl over an electric massager and it is not a euphemism
it roils beneath my shoulders like a hot tide, ripping gnarled knots of
muscle, myofascia, connective tissue webbed and croaking. I am doubling
the gabapentin dosage this week, and I am doubling my influx of iced
coffee with a splash of almond milk.

At the coffee shop next to my acupuncture clinic, the baristas see
me juggle laptop, phone, cane, wallet, headphones, coffee cup, cane,
metrocard, change they give me a free coffee as a good luck, free coffee as
a congratulations, free coffee because *you look so tired*, free coffee because I
know that they are people and I can handle our 10-second interaction like
the professional I was before my femmeness and my abject nerve pain got
in the way, the trickle of doubt that seized my shoulders in a tunnel of
slow aches, drawling surges, the kind you can't find or shake, that nothing
reaches that fades without noticing that you gave up trying to wind it
out, the wrongness of a body growing content to sting, relief at banded
cracked hand taking yours and pulling you into soundlessness, red light
bulb under tasseled shade, a warehouse thrumming dust, the only place
in North Carolina you can still smoke inside.

If I seem indifferent, it's my meds;
                    if I seem different, it's not me it's you
You, down and constant, cold and static even under quilt sewn of band
t-shirts, sand hurrying my bed like a fester, nest of lonely, drench of
gaunt, early morning crunchy stroll for coffee or a pastry or answers
to the questions your body carved into you like sliced cement, tarps of
melons frozen on thick paper, water, color.

Instead of looking, I learn to soften, wear red to support my root chakra, how I keep drawing the 10 of wands like some kind of fucking mantra *let something go let something go decide what you need and keep that let everything else flake off and flower elsewhere don't fight every fucking thing that leaves you be alone be good be good at being being alone good at be you leave being elsewhere off be thing good thing alone which thing alone and you*

You're forgiven, no matter what I've said on the street, in my bed, in your bed, by the river, against that building I said I would never forgive you well I am trying to and my therapist says I should let myself feel things and be okay with just feeling shit but I don't know about it I'd rather fester and remember everything, drag each slight around like a fucking anchor and finally scream and give up but that's an okay emotion to feel too.

Disappearing is harder than I remember.

ROT

In the window, an echo of sun: I lose you against the clouds, the
shade of ricocheting into corners, curled thighs a nest of calm, of
slatted wall
                              Instead of bending, we slip into each other
                and crest, edges of our chubby arms cherubic,
            splintered Against the odds, we experiment and come
        out glistening, parading Canal Street a slick eagle and
a grim leonine figure, glowering but

slim and long draped over trunk, her flattened body trembles green
against slumbering brush

When I come closer, she freezes, winnowing in breeze, leaves
whispering your name   brushing against the small hairs grown too
long behind my ears. I am   sprouting something small and
blonder than I expected, obfuscation against moon quipped
and relentless

holding firm against your   quavering haunches, slick with dew
blooming from your skin. If you were skinless, you'd still glisten like
a constellation

I trickle in; project unknowable. If you think of me as   vanishing,
I will become that for you. Against a
            greening sky, I can preen all I want.
in the end I am   emptying, becoming the vessel a gash drooping
with want. I could fit almost anywhere translucent as I am whole

Instead, picture me writhing somewhere warm, a car hood pooling
smoke against snow; the field excavated for homes where I grew up,
a reed-toothed dune

Nature is unnatural but I am in it anyway. Forgive me for what I
am about to say: that I can't live with myself if I let you walk away
unfinished, mouth mid-gape, smoke machine   belching fig
underground somewhere downtown. If I run from you, it's because I
know I can't hide anything in this dim rush of   throbbing light,
box tucked into corner and   humming

I make it natural, use my hands in new ways, press your body harder
and somehow I am still distant, a fleck of human in the mass of things
glooming in the sky, a handful of   glimmering rocks in salt, in
my palm as I loosen my hold on your coat, drape over a bench
overlooking the endless city,   thrumming beneath us, the water a
pool of things we can never know, things you silence me for
thinking;

I am worried for my self, my hands   becoming new creatures
    drenched in fur, in a warm skin
        warming more when I feel when I feel, I scurry to keep from
            unraveling, from emptying my insides into the bowl
                you hold out to me,   brimming
                    with something you claim is holy

POISON SEASON

When my name fills your mouth, it will leave you scorched, the
ruin I carry inside of me now your burden, your scarred hull
rueful as ever, I haunt you in slices of papers making claims, your
fringed throat a ghost, a ravaged edge

What is it about me that brings out the shrill violence in people?

OVERFLOW

The rheumatologist sizes me up, presses her soft hands into my
wound nest of a body, nothing unfurling under her hands like
it's supposed to. My cane looming lilac, my fifth appendage
I sprouted from a dream and allowed to fang into an organ,
tumorous and in bloom against concrete, shuffling stairwells,
flights and stationary things, a stability I forgot.

They draw a dozen vials of my warm indigo blood, streaking
crimson against curved glass jutting from the nurse's blue-gloved
fists, my platelets weapons. Everybody needs me but no one will
keep me. All the tests come back inconclusive : this doesn't make
me a mystery, just a stubborn femme, uncooperative flesh spilling
into public space, an occupation.

Piss ripples down my palms, I pinch the specimen container,
hoist my tote, palm my cane, slip down eggshell-lacquered hall,
turn over my bodyliquid, they will run a test and tell me why my
hands seize and curl, why pain trickles down from my skull like a
rain shower. *Stress hormones likely plentiful, obese and without distress.*

A CONSTANT

Wash the parts of me I fist to you, collide from neckbone down; if
again haunt trails, bemoan me then drip elsewhere edged monster,
your feathered crest radial, marrow glimmering where your
injections bloomed into pearls, turtling beach, jag the shells like
your story is only real insofar as it is salt

Beneath, I could swear American heart oils and hoards, your skin
swimming with flotsam, you're full of it; I know better, knits and
turtlenecks things I chose for myself, the way my belly chose its
permabloat, my filling and spilling a thing I remember but don't
believe

I believe victorious; how you held my hair like an object, how
when I said *fuck me* I meant leave; I couldn't say what I wanted: *you*
or *she* or *that one/this one, who I found draped in my small couch like a
grin, an arc of shrining silver, small pool awash on hardwood* but I spewed
anyway, stones doing their stoned heavy dance the way I know best

PART IV: MOLTING

I wake up unable to remember what my hands felt like when they could fold into soft shells; they are crispy as autumn branches, dried into curls brown as molasses. After a closing shift, my back gnarls into spirals of muscle, clenched against the server station fridge, opulent seasonal cakes and back stock of soy and almond milk suddenly looming, headstones for the weekend doubles and clopens I pulled without hesitation.

I spend the next morning in bed until I can't justify it to myself anymore, air conditioner humming, filling July humidity seeping in behind cheap cotton curtains.

I am really afraid of dying, which is why I spend so much time thinking about my body, how to carry it around, lined with regret and brittle muscle, edging bottom, wanting to just bruise and be done with it.

I keep trying to dissipate, but it is harder than it looks: dissolving. I don't remember what I used to do: waking up driving the speed limit on an eastern North Carolina highway, my front tire dipping into a rough just enough to render my metal skeleton immobile, my brain unfogging, anew.

The most of that body marked by edges, strong edges, something inside the strongest substance, firm but forgiving. I am filled by this, leaving room for almost nothing else, but I know you love the tiny empty part, the echo hiding somewhere inside, pearl in the gnarled shell of my body, its camouflage distinct and almost invisible.

When I tell my therapist that I am afraid of being weak, she asks what am I really afraid of and I cannot answer except to say *dependence, reliance, everyone thinking I'm a burden.* I unfold my cane in the waiting room, after I leave the small living room overlooking 60th Street with the rattling air conditioner, knowing that I don't want her to know, not yet, anyway.

HANDLE IT

Holding on, something else I cannot do, the cannonball wedged
between my shoulder blades an anachronism, marked by its age,
its inevitability, the way I already knew I was burning long before
I burned:

If I blame anyone, it's probably the echo of my blonded life frozen
in aging photos: me rapt with wine at an art show; me distant
with cigarette on downtown porch; me, a blur of warm aura, hair
curling, ringed with sweat. *Was it worth it* and I know it was, just
for the trickle of bodies up and down the long back stair to my
patio, the scald of Aristocrat vodka in a smoke-ravaged throat, the
warm crust of fresh fried donuts after a night of photo shoots.

Orthopedist slinking in to begin my week, pool of calendar days
to drown in, a holiday sparking a manic episode but in dreams
everything is smooth-edged and gentle, a classroom blooming
eager blossoms.

This relearning has come with practice: many weepy visits
to doctors' offices and therapy couches have left me equally
despondent and determined; weekly acupuncture appointments
get me spotty with cupping bruises and groggy from napping.

My green glass Mason jars swill with bitter brown tinctures of
ginseng for energizing, skullcap for headaches, fistfuls of red
jasper and tourmaline in my pocket support my root chakra;

I balm clove and sandalwood across my back for loosening, chamomile for spasms, maca for hormonal balancing; I bloom beargrass, jewelweed, my pothos tumbling an unimaginable forest, the tangle of my heating pads a jungle of buckwheat pillows and pill organizers.

WHAT I'M LOSING

Some nights a band tightens around my ribs, a closing I forgot
clenched me before but loosened with time, or by swallowing the
stretch of fascia, connective gunk lashing quixotic, inexplicable
except to cry for *rest* for *home*

The places my arms can't bend are the worst: lonely swatches
of bodyhunk bodythings backbody everybody needs to touch
their back once but only so much can be said for the closeness
of palming my own back, another thing I cannot do, the stripe I
paint across my heat a longitude for how the spine shrinks after
too long in bed

My speckled neck a reminder of what I'm losing; a sliver more
every day, flawed bodies are forgettable usually but how I am both
withering and widening is chipping away at me in ways foolish
and restless no settling, no forgiveness

This feels like how the film of sleep feels, it was there, feathers drifting
behind my shed skin, a mouthed creature visualizing itself gone

Good cry means moon, drenched, bathtub, fern draped down
shower like a web, taupe tile filling with resentment and breaking,
starting over, doing anything kick whistle yelp trail hold, hold

Moss

My attempts to draw water
from a wall of slate
have left my hands cracked.

In fairness, you warned me against
clawing: not here you said,
always hesitant to teach me
anything.

Miles deeper, moss blooms
pungent, emerald-wet, ripe
as new skin. Kneeling, I whisper

something like a prayer, before the language
of the day enters my body,
I sing hymns, fingers bleeding into
streams.

THIS IS NOT IN PRAISE OF POISONING MYSELF

after Jean-Michel Basquiat

I swallow the cap,
dream of anemones
again.

Everything is filled
with venom:

My mouth, your mouth,
kissing on the sidewalk,
swapping fang for fang.

I couldn't tell you then:
emerald is just black
before the sun sets.

Your fingers just can't
reach the sac pulsing
behind my molars.

This is not in praise of poison-
ing myself.

This is just to say,
I remember tendrils,

my hands full
of sloughed skin.

Night is a jewel
I whisper your name into.

THE POOL II

Long live Thursdays, gentle thrum of tide on old wood, crossing
the bridge to drip young

Front door a poison, knob slick with split where it should have
been cool cinderblock

What are we made of? A knocking prevails, windows cracked low
key, quiet urge to transform, unignorable and long-haired, blood
bath between my teeth, lips rimmed with salt speck

My fist for your eyelash, a ride for a gulp; you call me by my new
name, leave me hooked on the back of your closet, street wear,
that night in the pool, naked crust of moon held underwater,
the ground leaking the hormones my blood couldn't balance, my
organs slurped like milkshakes

When my brow slips you know I am low on forgiveness, relentless
push towards horizon unknowable, alone in the study making
calls, my feet bare against rough grass, fireflies, rope hammock
curving under my hips, belting my jeans higher

I took whatever I could

my hands on because you were in the room

MELT

Call me mothering, catch me aflutter feathering knife, satchel,
green dead grass, Knut Hamsun heavy in back pocket, heavy as
days crimped with lawlessness.

House melt: puddle-beginning, pool of need, my blood or
another toxic wet thing, warming on a warm day. Let it go or
gnash your hands like arcs, like ships grim and gray, hillocks
dredging hope, hopelessness prevailing.

If I tell you to move on, I am cruel but I am actually soft inside
this husk of hardened no's the noisiness of putting my boots away,
pitting cherries over kitchen sink already slick with detergent, grief

TASTE ME AS A WAY OF BEING ME

after Grace Krilanovich

By the time you let me sleep, it is already morning.

When you sleep, you purr like a nice girl, your
little motor, our legs rustling in the soft
nook of your bed, your hair everywhere.

Clean your room for me, wash the mug
I leave on the bookshelf and make
a big deal out of it. When I cry after fucking, it's not you.

I am a closed door, sealed vat of blood and brain always a flurry.

If there was a question of where I go, you would have to
ask another chamber, dim screen, kneeler
sticky in confessional, my robes discarded.

Mornings, I pull on your shirt, drag you
out of bed like an animal, wolf claws flexing over your
glistening flank.

Our mutual language:
       ocean, grief untraceable,
a perpetual mourning for totally
different things

Handsome men act
like they already know
me: familiar rakishness,
spatial entitlement,
willingness to interrupt—
I am their brother and
they are frightened and
intrigued, soft butch
novelty

My body is not under attack from anyone but myself

PART V:
TOUGHNESS

ANOTHER CONSTANT

Choose me, I am writing about hollowing houses again, dreaming
about hollows, house, a gain

however slippery, dumping drawers into clear trash bags, sorrow a
constant

Is there other firsts we can esteem here like gentle, echo above
rippled rock, the casting off

I am pumped full of stuff: toughness, tender spots (like a little
flicker in my heart), vessels of

Stone Femme Blues

The first day I wear platform shoes, I fall down walking to the train. I am always thinking about this: how my body can't take another fall; brittle at 27, drained. My plastic flatform sandals squeak as I walk, and the sole catches on a patch of uneven sidewalk. It doesn't even register that I am falling until I drop my cane and my knees hit concrete, my voluminous skirt pillowing out above my compression socks. Skin. Sidewalk. I am 10 yards from my train stop and everyone has seen me fall. I scurry to my feet and hurry underground, my knees stinging, my palms shaking from the impact.

At work, my wisdom teeth hurt so much. I don't have a prescription for painkillers but I probably should, the way my face feels like a stone wall sinking, how my shoulders are stone, my throat rimmed with stone, heavier and harder all the time.

Last night, the skin beneath my tits, the top of my stomach, was so tight, I couldn't breathe. The smaller, newer of our two cats was sneezing a lot and I rolled out of bed to check on her, get her fresh water. As I knelt down to run their ears, it felt like I had been stabbed under my left breast, between my ribs. I gasped, stunned, like I'd been punched, my solar plexus frozen in a spasm.

At the edge of your map, you crimp into singular unit, developing spine, blossoming brave: leap into air, youngling, and trickle down, a leaf clamoring against gravity.

I will
not give up.

ANOTHER CONDITIONAL

If something goes to the bone, it is thought to be deep; what is
beneath bone? More meat, more gunk, more bodyodyody to get
unforgiven, cantankerous, needing a seat with a back like for sure
the sudden rain drenching the warm health I felt urging in my
skin, pillows foam shields, looking for friends no longer there,
being able to happen

Stop trying, even when you've gone dry. You know better than
to collect my shards and cast them into something sphered,
something sober

When I tell you *I'm tired* you make me wait like a dog

You think you want to take care of me but you don't. This doesn't
make you bad the way that other things might: I get it, loving
and resenting me, how I can suck the youth out of any room once
you look at me with sad eyes over something fucking absurd that
you *knew* was a joke I scorch everything with my teeth, my loud
mouth a coal soaking rage, wrath, gutsquirm

A Savage Lesson in Letting Go

One must consent to burning
   — Antonin Artaud

Instead of pushing back, you phone it in, melon sky sinking heavy
with rain, clouds the whitest thing about today. Summer blooms
from my concrete roof, I text you an explanation of my silence,
how the cord spools diagonally across your chest, hypotenuse.

Still, I fixate on your in pieces: which clump embodies my desire
today, in early sun, demands it? Eventually you are a million
flakes of self, unfair reduction, fragments of a subject, looming
towards whole.

The first girl I put my fingers into has a two-year-old and half-
sleeves of black roses and skulls, her dead dad's name in script. We
poured Skittles into Smirnoff, torched safety pins with lighters
pocketed at the stab-n-grab after the punk show, before the
graveyard. I could stay with her, the TV an indigo hum, cigarettes
tucked behind our ears, bleach scalding pale hairlines. Instead, I
cut my bangs, settled for sad guys into butt stuff: (a savage lesson
in letting go:
your body unbroken, you don't need my spine,
your smoky panels marking the beginning of forgiving yourself)

If no one was there to watch us, we'd cut into everything, auto-
dismemberment, auto-erotic, each other's shadows with new names.

Each tiny betrayal, the reveal of abandonment, the life of the body still a nightmare. I break my heart, hoping it will swell enough to make a cave for you, a nest of blood and bass, escape.

Not everything I do is good.

I am inside my body, inside your body, but it matters less and less.

My rough promises are, like my forgiveness, non-negotiable, sure as a stone smoothing after years tumbling in a peacoat pocket, sleeves wide enough for my hands to scrabble into your elbow and rest against the thrum of your blood, my own ventricles awash, safe.

Tell me you've found something new beside the green hill, stone arch above Brooklyn Lake, looming south, bridges trussed like crests past edges of our endless island. It's a sin, to leave here without a goodbye, a final push for togetherness, even as we peel wool cardigans and soft cottons from our shoulders, basking in days stretching longer again, the last snow of the year freckling the industrial strip between your apartment and the D train.

When I mourn my self, it is not grief I call upon.

ANOTHER DRAWL

I see two things in the blue your body gulps: roundness, cooling
violet, a dry sadness scraped away into shards of your autumn
skins, your haunch a fishing village aflame with line and shadow

The way a vineyard does more than bloom, the timbre of October
loosening, parquet floors sprinkled with flecks of storm water, a
frill of canvas sopping in the foyer.

You couldn't begin to see the cartography of my desire: ruched
and augmented, crackling haughty noise, ankle pooling out of
boot, legs spread open, knees draped caverns, folded map of my
self burned around its soft edges

Soft Notes

: the kind we made beneath slivered west-fronted window, a gaze
un-

I want to fight until I am no longer cold, till fire can fan itself in
my guts, the places that throbs underneath my breasts, the way
I am ever-expanding, a universe of getting sick at inappropriate
times, needing help more all the time, of so many cute mugs and
so long alone on the subway between work and everything else,
how I prescribe everyone herbs and then cure them with my hands
but can't cure myself.

Mercy, kite spiralling, verbs are the things I want to go to, how
do you know the difference between gaunt and execution how do
I tell my students that white america wants to leave them behind
can we please glimpse humanity of brown people why can't white
people get our shit together

Unbranded gentle, clean canvas creased and sewn shut, my flap of
a mouth unflappable; observing a phenomenon renders it unreal,
a simulacrum of itself, a shadow backlit onto a sheet draped
across piano wire, our birthday party in a Cambridge basement,
air steeped late July, color pooling into your five-bedroom
apartment, drained of bodies for the summer months.

Back then, my body was forgiving: late nights capped with roof
cigarettes and windy rides in borrowed cars, hair drenched in city
light, stereo, a softer look at things gone awry

Another Monday Where I Think I Have Borderline Personality Disorder

I can't get my mood under control, can't make eye contact. I just
learned that I've been dissociating when I have panic attacks, and
that this has likely been happening for over a decade. When I was
14, I used to cut myself with tweezers, the sharp, accurate kind
from the name-brand column of the cosmetics aisle. I obsessively
read *YM* and am trying to figure out my brows, how to keep
eyeliner from smearing, hiding dark lipstick in the front pockets
of my faux-leather jacket that I wear every day. Now, nag champa
and oily peanuts situate me cross legged on my full-size futon,
my stereo jangling with 70s punk, a mixtape from my internet
boyfriend. This was the first time it happened: I had just cut my
hair short and it would stay that way pretty consistently for the
rest of my life, rough dishrag in my lap, I drag the arrived edge
of the tweezers across my left forearm, a soft white canvas
blooming with slits of blood, jagged pooling, how I clean up
right away, but not before I feel an aggressive blend of relief and
vanishing. I am a kid and I am unbelievably sad and I don't want
to die, not yet,
but almost.

PART VI:
A FEMME INCANTATION

THE NECKLACE

In the case of you forgetting I want off the hook goodness you know the kind
you don't trim up and split the kind that gives gunk and floors gasp or spit

but hey don't forget when I left gargantuan I didn't yet from the fleeced
beck of slick cloud how I left it to you or dreamt another any other also for

when you haunt hidden nerve bit and how the wind fingers knowing-
ness, a hound gripping bike lock or something whispered outside coffee house

I left everything there with you, how the coast crushed me and made me feel
guilty for it how flimsy grade sidewalk crimp sold me a faulty start, a dim

slender jaunt kick over yesterday dawn mammal, you fur, gent sheen,
feather me today the way we used to glim emerald shimmered lamplight,

your candle-drenched low ceiling a tasseled draped you hunched like
a cinderella three mattresses one electric outlet strings of dreams in the open

closet you hung coats foresting entryway, your cave a forgotten jubilant I
remember you like this: a lil glum, lot young lot flippant lot strung

lot taut lil heart lot wing, you stretching shoulder glint, stars still
tender, tattoo of atlas moth tuck intact however jaundiced reel me in

by talking more slice a cute angle, femme gutter, how will you find me
again once I am blonde again, that boring party, same news as last year,

you know the one with the hand sewn collar, the slow like molasses slow
move towards your mouth on my cheap couch, window aghast onto alley

When I say I am writing about love, I really mean that I am still looking
for a word that means *tightening* in the way that love makes you tighten,

but also *unspool* like bespoke yarn left in summer shower, *tenderness* like
that sliver of fat you know the one you like under my armpit, *float* like

when everything tides away like mist and your face is what's left of the
wreckage, the mess I made by not leaving bed until I couldn't stand

the ache of sinking by body a fucking anchor I neglect to cast off from
the light of parties in emptied corrals, warehouses, industrial needless

hemming, starling awash I want to leave it on until it turns my skin green

It's Not Gonna Kill You

hawk, jagged insides, chemical-drift, the lisped roundness of your
scoop neck soft shirt the one you wore on the roof as the moon
licked your neck curled behind you like a small mammal how your
fur was drenched with bonfire, knee-high reeds

I can't be sweet, I'd rather tell you in advance, the way your cheek
purples with regret the only guiding light I ever needed wait
actually I'm sweet when we're alone and I've toed my boots under
your desk with a thunk

I believed you always

Get stoned and listen to music by my best friends I meant to write
dead but I wrote best but I really meant dead

How dead is nothing more than inertness, a wool coat emptied

ISO Femme Top

I just wanna be liberated
    — Kanye West

If we are anything, we are mismatched, making up for each other's emptiness.

I rattle, gush and curl, wrap across your hips and vanish in a web of blood and static, spitting grime and surge. You flash beige carpeting and disappear, quell my search with a whispered nothing, *you love me*, you want to know what places make me sad.

Anywhere crowded, I say, knowing that New York was not meant for me, claustrophobic and agoraphobic wallowing together in paralysis, paroxysm, the fantasy of you with any other girl, your mouth full of moonstone, mine full of your skin.

Instead of forgiveness, let's try opening. I confess I can't go anywhere, my heels cracked into blisters, blood, bone sharding in my boot; not only that, but I freeze and hide in strangers' houses, unable to find a seat, I duck out the back door to smoke, March defiantly crisp, my nails full of silt from clutching every surface until my fingers crack.

If I could turn me off, I would. I don't want to come so fast, to need so much, begging to be filled, ISO femme top, tall, bossy, but also nice and smart, into witchy stuff, poems, also lite d/s maybe, tryna get beat up a lil bit but also self-care

Anyway, pitted against everything, I cannot curl far enough into the corner where you tucked my jeans, or someone's jeans, my t-shirt wet with come and your mouth full again of saliva, the way you gargle it in the night, a canto for my aching wrists.

Palm

Invite strangers in,
front gate dangling
like a tooth.

I never learned
to budget

Scrub maple floor
with your palms,
rinse
and hold me

I HAVE THIS THING WHERE I'M NOT AFRAID OF ANYTHING BECAUSE BAD THINGS HAVE HAPPENED TO ME

after Lorelei Ramirez

The more I drink, the more I remember how much I have to lose,
the way shelves do more than rim, how they flood with numbered
boxes, gerunds deployed iffily, a casket redundant and jaunty,
a languid cage, pothos unspooling dreamily, patchwork a field
afront or lined

When I remember how I am a fern, I know I've dreamt an
unforgivable stench, floodlight, willy-nilly, accompaniment a
succulent, trembling stacked plate stacked cup stacked small saucer

I will find the other Leo at the party and show off with them,
preen and flip my hair, femme dandy and show up just late
enough to make an entrance; catch me garlic gleam, sharp
sweetness pillowing between my molars, aching immortal, clean
begotten, lipstick on my teeth like a trashcan

Aghast, your Afghan tumbles elsewhere, how everything was
a knotted mess of performances of spider plants, a service dog
nesting in my folded arms, the way you tie your scarf a myth of
delicious birdcage, knotty vines undergird lapel, round lake, I fall
down the stairs and allow hanker for nori, for southern exposed
throat or bumblebee, a shrug, a happening, a tooth loosed

Try me: I had a shadow before this stool, drown or go home, my skirt slicing into buttock, hillock

Tell me again how I'd grim you, how I'd flaunt small breasts like a fantasy if I had them, a *could* long lingering, bread crust braided into my hair like a flagship, an excess of lip balm congealing into the corners of my mouth, yawning, aghast, thin t

You can kill whenever you want

PART VII:
THE FINAL ONE

No emotion is the final one
— Jeanette Winterson

If I've learned anything, it was starting somewhere, allowing
for nostalgia, embracing the fantasy that warm days form: the
knowing, the final one, the falling

That was okay, launch or kick or wasting time, the surge of
slippery lampweed lit by firefly, the ones you bottled gently in your
dream, your yard aflame with bonfire, my body a whirl of floral,
skirts, a femme spinning

It's a little more than gentle, instead a surge of fluster, huddle
slimmed by seasons, ripples in a pond or whatever put my hand
back in your pocket so I can remember what I lost in the first place,
the voluminousness of what I'm hiding inside of you, in how you
dry the plates badly

The sink held more bowls than we ever chose together, dusty
Salvation Army shelves stickered with the gunk of stuff you left
behind,

There is no work that isn't wet work; instead, voluminous,
elaborate borage done kaput yet how before begun some dip ecstatic

Get ecstatic, grind yr gears yr gunk grind it get loblolly in this
bitch go rigid go topple go slump distraught

How could I drop the memory of you: armfuls of apple,
mcintosh, crab

When I tell you the difference between male and female crabs you can't believe I know as much as I do about estuaries, that I ever took my shoes off in nature but I did back when it mattered to me, to crab, to net a full load of seagunk

A straight girl asks me how many tattoos I have but in a whisper like she's scared to find out; as I count them by touching them through my clothes she can't believe it I can't believe she can't believe it but she asks anyway I say I will pull down the leg of my leggings right here if you want let me know how you're feeling about it, how my shorts are always splattered with wetness from my nerves unable to regulate my body temperature I'm just more sensitive my doctor says and poison is so much more than where I laid my limp eager body eager for thirst and drowned by pollen gargaunt, ignoble:

Pour directly into the wound, the flagrant cast iron hydrophilic urge of my body, the way it rusts but loves the slow growth of an earthy crust like a dry summer an empty beach a gone serpent

Empty it into the bucket I store in my body the one you can fill with round stones until I forget my name, have you make me the bed, float into it a salt breeze,

molt: my final form is forgettable but blue like seaglass

ACKNOWLEDGMENTS

This book would not exist without the relentless support of my queer family, especially Robin Reid, Donte, Andréa, Chett, Everest, and Zefyr.

I love you I love you I love you.

To mentors who've emerged from ruinous institutions with grace and humor: Carmen, Tom, Kirk, Katherine, Deaver, Kandice, and others to come.

Gratitude to my parents for fomenting my Leo femme power, sometimes despite themselves. The magnetic pull of femme-for-femme is strong, and I am relentlessly awed by how we show up sparkling.

Super grateful to disability Twitter for their infinite good politics and advice.

Thanks to Bryan and Seth for their care, generosity, and bolstering emails, and to my sweet blurbers who offered up wisdom, incisive notes, and so much femme power.

Gratitude to the editors of the following publications, where many of these poems first appeared:

"ISO Femme Top" in *Dream Pop Press*

"Argonaut" in *Agape Editions*

"Drag" in *Pigeonholes*

"The Final One" in *SCUM*

"Rain, Glitter, Rain" and "Molting" in *Monstering*

"The Pool I," "The Pool II," "A Conditional," and "Another Conditional", and "Another Drawl" in *The Rotting Kind* (Ghost City Press, 2017)

"Taste me as a way of being me" in *Moonsick Magazine*

"Bone Stuff," "More Like a Saga," and "What I'm Losing" in *The Wanderer*

"Tender Limbs" in *Crab Fat Magazine*

"It's Not Gonna Kill You" in *Vagabond City*

"Genesis" and "Drawl" in *Black Napkin Press*

"Cervical Traction" and "How to be Impressive" in *tenderness yea*

"A Conditional" in *occulum*

"Overflow" in *Deaf Poets Society*

"Overflow" republished in *Rising Phoenix*

"Another Conditional" in *Bad Pony*

"The Pool II" and "Another Drawl" in *Public Pool*

"The Uninhabitable" in *Perigee: Apogee*

"The Pool" in *Seafoam Magazine*

"Better Skin" in *Love My Belly Zine*

"Handle It" in *Lavender Review*

"Muffle" in *Thistle Magazine*

"Then You See It" in *HOLD: A Journal*

About the Poet

Jesse Rice-Evans (she/her/hers) is a queer femme rhetorician and doctoral student at the CUNY Graduate Center researching intersections of language, disability, and digital culture. She is the author of several chapbooks; this is her first full-length collection. Find her at jessericeevans.com.

About the Press

Sibling Rivalry Press is an independent press based in Little Rock, Arkansas. It is a sponsored project of Fractured Atlas, a nonprofit arts service organization. Contributions to support the operations of Sibling Rivalry Press are tax-deductible to the extent permitted by law, and your donations will directly assist in the publication of work that disturbs and enraptures. To contribute to the publication of more books like this one, please visit our website and click *donate*.

Sibling Rivalry Press gratefully acknowledges the following donors, without whom this book would not be possible:

Tony Taylor	Russell Bunge
Mollie Lacy	Joe Pan & Brooklyn Arts Press
Karline Tierney	Carl Lavigne
Maureen Seaton	Karen Hayes
Travis Lau	J. Andrew Goodman
Michael Broder & Indolent Books	Diane Greene
Robert Petersen	W. Stephen Breedlove
Jennifer Armour	Ed Madden
Alana Smoot	Rob Jacques
Paul Romero	Erik Schuckers
Julie R. Enszer	Sugar le Fae
Clayton Blackstock	John Bateman
Tess Wilmans-Higgins & Jeff Higgins	Elizabeth Ahl
Sarah Browning	Risa Denenberg
Tina Bradley	Ron Mohring & Seven Kitchens Press
Kai Coggin	Guy Choate & Argenta Reading Series
Queer Arts Arkansas	Guy Traiber
Jim Cory	Don Cellini
Craig Cotter	John Bateman
Hugh Tipping	Gustavo Hernandez
Mark Ward	Anonymous (12)

www.ingramcontent.com/pod-product-compliance
Lightning Source LLC
Chambersburg PA
CBHW022037090426
42741CB00007B/1103